Good Brown Girls

poems & experiences
by Parul L. Bhandari

Apne (Our People)

To the girl who walks to her own *dhol* (drum),
ears adorned in *jhumkas,*
I see you.

To the girl who speaks in multiple tongues,
mouth adorned with a lip fringe,
I see you.

To the girl who stops water,
filling drains and envy cups with her long hair,
I see you.

To the girl who brings the spice,
and always adds chili flakes,
I see you.

To request permission, contact the publisher at:
publisher@innerpeacepress.com

ISBN: 979-8-90221-997-2
Good Brown Girls

May 2026

Printed in U.S.A.

Published by Inner Peace Press
Eau Claire, Wisconsin
www.innerpeacepress.com

For my mothers, aunts, sisters, and friends...
who have shown me strength and acceptance...

You have guided the way.

Chapters

one:
anjaan
(unknown)

A selection of stories about self-discovery, growth, and newness. *Anjaan* refers to an unknown person, and in it's truest form is not known by one's heart.

Good Brown Girls

Be a good girl.
Carry in the tea.

Be a good student.
Only A's, no B's.

Be a good worker.
Only in some careers.

Be a good wife.
Never give them tears.

Be a good mother.
Model their worth.

Be a good daughter.
Carry their torch.

Be a good girl,
By their ideal.
Pray, Cook, Work, Bow, and Yield.

Be a **Good Brown Girl.**

Padharo Sa

("Welcome in" in Mardwadi)

Welcome in...
Your journey awaits.
From desert to tundra,
Your story creates.

Welcome in...
Your journey is long.
From *Bharat* to *Am'rika.*
Your anxieties are not wrong.

Welcome in...
To a foreign land,
From *desh* to country.
You're beginning to understand.

Welcome in...
There is room for all.
But, know that you are different.
And try not to fall.

Khata Mheeta

"Sweet and Sour"

I don't know how to date.
I never was allowed to.

I don't know how to cope.
I never was taught to.

I don't know how to speak love.
I never was spoken to.

I don't know how to disrespect.
I never dared to.

I don't know how to say no.
I never tried to.

I don't know where to learn.
Or how to learn.

Shiny strappy sandals,
Peeled off swollen feet.
Toes throb from the pressure,
Dancing feet loved the beat.

Sequins on a blouse,
Scrape skin when removed.
Arms burn with red streaks,
These limbs had swayed and moved.

Bangles colorful and clinking,
Scratch hands as they slide through.
Hands swollen from salty *paneer*,
And a drink or two.

Earrings with thick posts of gold,
Leave tender holes.
Earlobes sting, red and burdened.
Sounds had opened up the souls.

Makeup thick and sticky,
Wipes away rough.
Skin soft and puffy.
Lips pink from the buff.

At the end of the night.
As it all comes off,
Beat by beat.
Piece by piece,

A sense of relief decends...
while the marks remain.

The Girl at the Wedding

Who am I?
A brown girl, raised in the heart of the US.
Riddled with shame for the black hair on my legs.
Beaming from praise for the black hair on my head.

Who am I?
The kid with all A's.
Riddled with guilt over wanting to be something else.
Beaming with praise when I got their degree.

Who am I?
A good Indian daughter, with a rebellious streak.
Riddled with lies and secret "friends."
Beaming with joy when finally "settling down."

Who am I?
A minority in my country.
Riddled with guilt over the privileges I have.
Beaming with pride for the privileges we built.

Who am I?
A bundle of people, culture, and emotions.
Riddled with guilt and tradition.
Beaming with pride and *sanskar.*

The Seekers
(aka the Marriage Mart)

Senses,
Drunk off the hype,
Hungry for more.
Scan the ~~room~~ screen.

The sweet-talker
The smooth-walker.
The sharp dresser.
The bank account.

Their man, their world, their mind.
Doctor. Lawyer. Engineer. Tech Bro.

Only here can you believe.
Only here can you succeed.
Only here do the strong survive.

Find the key to your ring,
or leave empty-handed.

Denial

Discussions we never have.
Words open, thoughts unspoken.
We should talk.
Eventually, we will talk.

Passwords we never shared.
Accounts locked. Plans left open.
We should discuss it all.
Eventually, we will discuss.

Emotions we never realized.
Feelings blocked, words choked.
We should share them.
Eventually, we will share.

Discussions we never had.
Denial rules this space.
There will be time still.
Eventually, we will.

14

*(this is your cue to say the thing,
do the thing, talk about the things...)*

Pressure

Make-up on a face,
Too made up for her own good.

"Wear lipstick so they notice you."

It screams so loud.

What does it cover?
Is it pain? Is it hope?

Clothes on a body.
Shrouding something more.

"Wear something so they see you."

What do these clothes hide?
Is it pride? Is it deprevation?

They hide the truth.

Shades over eyes.
Too scared for her own good.

"Cover what you don't want to show."

What do those eyes hide?
Is it power? Is it fear?

Though the influence may be real,
Covering up to cover.

What lies behind it,
May be lost.

two:
pehchan
(recognizing)

A selection of tales about finding
greater understanding in oneself.
The deeper meaning of *pehchan*
is to know someone, or at least be
acquainted with them.

Pardesi Woman

(foreign woman)

What could she have been?
The lady in a *sari*,
head covered and hunched.
Always serving men.

What could she have been?
The budding businesswoman,
mind filled with ideas.
Words stifled by custom.

What could she have been?
The muted mathematician,
shrewd and calculating.
Counting the price of vegetables, not stocks.

What could she have been?
The potential teacher,
always helping others.
Only allowed to teach her own.

Who did she become?
The lady who left,
she traveled far and over oceans.
Carrying tradition and creating her own.

Who did she become?
The doer.
She cooked, she taught, she calculated, she built.
Developing herself and her future.

Who did she become?
The chooser.
Not the life she could have had, but the life she made.
Crafting and creating something better.

Who did she become?
All the things and more.
A woman in a foreign land where opportunity stood.
Who rose and seized the day.

The Spice Trade

Aromas abound, we all smell of it.
Turmeric, ginger, cumin, and chili.
It reddens my face when friends come by.
While it fulfills my soul.

Recipes unwritten, measured by instinct.
A pinch of *asafoetida* is all you need.
It perplexes me when I try to replicate them.
While providing constant comfort.

Tongues tingling, heightened by heat.
Crunchy, salty, spicy, and sweet.
It tempts me when its time to dine.
And satiates like nothing else.

Steam rising, dishes on dishes.
Aunties recipes, learned from their aunties.
It permeates constant competition,
While it binds community ties.

Spices make a colorful array.
While tins hold recipes of heart,
Passed down. Raised up. Rooted.
The most perfect trade.

Pass the Chili

The steam rose from the warm rice, white and fluffy. It tickled her nose when she opened the rice cooker lid. "Perfect rice comes only from the rice cooker for me," she thought.

As she went to set the table, she made sure to bring plates, spoons, bowls, and napkins. And of course, the chili flakes and hot sauce.

No meal could ever be complete without it. Even as a girl who did not "eat much spice," it was a staple in her home, fridge, and table.

She plated the vegetables and *dal*, atop a mounain of rice. As everyone got their food, the first words rang out.

"Pass the chili."

A phrase so simple and yet so telling.

A phrase so common, yet something uncommon outside their walls.

A phrase so important, that they traveled with hot sauce on trips.

To come from the land of spice and sizzle means to make chili your companion.

What was most interesting though, was having to ask for it over and over.

At the pizza place they always frequent, "could you please bring chili flakes?"

At the Asian spot in the neighborhood, "can you please bring the chili oil?"

At the Tex-Mex place down the street, "can you please bring the really hot salsa?"

She looked around the table, at the people who had adapted to their lives here. Speaking English and wearing American clothes. Now a few generations in, and not uncommon to be seen.

And yet...

...who still had to ask for the chili wherever they went.

Her Mark

I always notice them.

A red bindi on the side of my mother's mirror.
A green bindi on the car rearview.
A gold bindi in the bathroom.
Black bindi in her handbag.

Reminiscent of that day.
Marking a moment.

The mark of a ~~married~~ woman.
The sign of her culture.
The color of her clothes.

I always notice the bindi.
Stuck on a frame.
A relic of time.

And I know, my mother was there.

Worthy

She is too skinny, arms like a flamingo's legs.
Feed her more.
Prick.

She is too fat, built like a bear.
Feed her less.
Prick.

She is too tall, neck like a girrafe.
Make her hunch.
Prick.

She is too small, she looks like a child.
Make her stretch.
Prick.

Who will marry her?
What will they say?
What will we do?
Prick, prick, prick.

Who decides?
Who cares?

She is human, she feels each prick.

She is person, pain grows from each kick.

She is woman, guilt builds with each nick.

She is worthy of more.

*Go ahead, cut out this page,
and use it when you need it.
Give it to those who measure
your worth in pounds.*

The blackest black.
Lined brown eyes.
Thick and smooth.
They sell and they smold.

The perfect orb.
Clear and white.
Almond shaped,
And oh so bright.

The deepest brown.
Irises so bold.
Deep and round.
What stories do they hold?

The softest brush.
Lashes long.
Touch high cheeks,
And spin envy like gold.

Mature yet naive.
Sensitive yet sharp.
Seeing yet knowing.

Brown Eyed Girl

Chai Time

The practice, steeped and sweet.
Water, leaves, spice, sugar.
Brings joy and routine,
Warmth and caffeine.

The ritual, calm and concentrated.
Cups, biscuits, saucers, and spoons.
Brings peace and calm,
A soothing daily balm.

The taste, bitter and bright.
Masala, ginger, milk, and water.
Awakens the senses,
A retreat from your defenses.

The event, lively and rich.
Tea, friends, chats, and more.
Brings constant connection,
A perfect affection.

The Cycle

Blood red, blood.
It brought with it pain.
The first signs of womanhood
and "life as we know it"...
Burdening pain.
At just 10 years old.

Blood red, blood.
It brought with it pleasure.
The first act of womanhood.
Sharp pain then pleasure.
At just 20 years old.

Blood red, blood.
It brought with it relief.
The bane of young womanhood, prevented.
Pulsing pain, welcome this time.
At just 25 years old.

Blood red, blood.
It brought with it sadness, loss.
Failure of womanhood.
Pain and stress, stress and pain.
At just 30 years old.

Blood red, blood.
It brought with it happiness.
The goal of womanhood.
Labored pain. And new life.
At just 35 years old.

Blood red, blood… lost.
It should have been joyful,
But was filled with heat.
The end of womanhood.
Pain, fire, pain, and then nothing.
At just 50 years old.

Blood and pain,
Pain and blood,
The "cycle" is life.
It always remains.

Aunty's

What should I wear?
White or black?
A *sari* or a dress?
Sounds frivolous,
But the question is true.

It's my first real sense of loss.

I remember going to Aunty's house for *pujas,*
Or pizza Fridays.
She always served soda,
Even for *Durga puja,*
when she placed a big red dot on my head.
She served soda later.

It's my first real funeral.

I remember hearing about funerals.
I remember hearing about loss.
But, I never really knew it.

I knew Aunty.
Aunty would feed me rice with ghee and sugar,
When I stayed for dinner.

Funeral

She spoke sweetly and softly, like a mouse.
She was as shrewd as she was naive.
She called me *beta*.

Like my mom.

It's the first time death feels close.

Aunty, and the other aunties,
Were part of our lives as long as we had been.
Forever.

Aunty and Mom met ages ago.
They were like sisters, who loved and hated each other.
They lived parallel lives, emulated and envied.

It's the first time loss feels real.

I wish I had a plain white *kurta*.
Why don't I have a plain white *kurta*?
What should I wear?

The Indo-Americans

"The only brown kid in class,"
Was not a novel phrase.

Aunties and Uncles were family,
Who were raised in completely different ways.

Those walking into your home,
Were greeted by onion and caraway.

Indian friends and American friends,
Were how we played.

Indian things and American things.
Marked our dual ways.

First generations of first generations,
Learning more day by day.

Children of immigrant engineers and business owners,
Now doctors and MBAs.

They came to the land of opportunity,
Come what may.

Trying to hold on to the old.
While evolving day by day.

Break Ups

They said,
    It wouldn't take so long,
    It wouldn't be this way,
    I would move on, eventually.

You said,
    It wouldn't last this long,
    It couldn't work,
    I would move on, eventually.

I said,
    It's not fair.
    It's too fast.
    I can't move on.

three:
kaam
(work)

Anecdotes on those working
to sustain or grow people, careers,
purpose, and passion.

Kaam refers to the work we do,
wherever we are, and whatever our role.

Sounds of Modern Motherhood

First sound, "shots fired, more bad news…"
I shudder.
My morning news alarm.
What a lovely world.

Second sound, "Mamaaaa,"
I scramble.
The baby is up.
Fed and changed, all before chai.

Third sound. Brushes buzzing.
I run to make breakfast.
Served and carried,
with side of *desi* guilt.

Fourth sound. Cars honking.
I rush to the car line,
Only to wait, and be late.

Fifth sound, calls and muted zooms.
I smile for the camera.
My "work" smile and practiced poise.
Work performances tried and true.

Sixth sound. Cars again.
I rush into school.
Mid-day *Diwali* crafts.
Making magic while on a balance beam.

(American-Born Conscious Desi version)

ABCD is common ethnic slur for American-born
"confused" *desis* not born in their homelands.

Seventh sound. The zooms connect.
I head home again.
Meetings in the car will have to do.
Career with a culture break.

Eighth sound. Sizzles and steam.
I hustle to prep dinner.
Rotis and *dal*. Frozen *dal*.
"You don't cook enough."
(At least it's Indian food.)
Dinner with another side of good old *desi* guilt.

Ninth sound. Bollywood songs and brushing.
I shuffle through the routine.
Who has mental space still?
(At least we read.)
Bedtime for the weary parent.

Tenth sound. The TV clicks on.
I relish the moment.
It's hard to do much more.
(At least we do it together.)
Mindless time = quality time.

And repeat.

Chosen

How was I chosen for my life? I had never thought about it before.

I was a mish-mash – a brown kid, growing up in middle class white America in the 1980s. My day-to-day resembled much of my midwestern upbringing, with a sprinkling of Indian food and Hindi school on Sunday. I danced like other young girls my age, only I took *bharatnatyam* in the conference room of a hospital. I traveled for school holidays too. Only we didn't go to Florida for a week every year instead went to India for the whole... hot... summer.

This was one of those "vacations."

As soon as I stepped off the plane, I smelled "India." It's a smell my nose had stored away as a little memory to unlock on these occasions. It smelt a bit of damp, of sweat, of spice, mixed in with dirt and coconut oil all in one.

Boy, it was hot. Super hot. Though we were in an "air conditioned" airport and you could feel the heat seeping through the cracks in the marble.

"Everything is always marble," I thought. "It keeps you cooler, I think, I suppose."

The marble was white and yellow, and brown sometimes. There were bright orange chairs in the waiting areas, which were a pop compared to the dingy yellowish-white floors. By the orange chairs and orange podiums, there were pictures of the Air India mascot greeting us as we exited.

In the bathroom there were stalls with white hole toilets – is that what they are called? It should be. There was a broom closet open on the right with a small mat on the floor surrounded by cleaning supplies. As we walked into the bathroom, a woman walked out of one of the stalls with a mop – "*Aap jao*" – she said. "You go in."

I thought more about the mat. It was her place to rest. Did she spend her life in the bathroom? Did she live here? Was she married? Who would marry the toilet girl?

I almost fell backwards in my squat, as I was lost in thought, but caught myself on the water nozzle. I grasped and remembered, no toilet paper. Ugh. It was going to be a long two months in India.

I have Paruresis, a fear of public toilets without any medical cause. At least I do right now. And I will be stressing about going to the bathroom in India for the rest of the next two months.

Ok, I may not have Paruresis but I likely have IBS, so India can be a cruel place to my stomach. Over the years I have visited family here and often spent many days curled up in a bed not feeling well.

As I washed my hands, I was reminded of the last trip when I avoided the dreaded "shot" – the one which scars your arm forever. It's a thing.

I followed my mom and sister out of the bathroom, and listened as they talked about the bathrooms in India disappointedly. Even my mom, who had grown up in India, had gotten used to the cushy American toilet system, and was not thrilled by the bathroom.

As we walked through the massive marble halls, going to grab our massive Samsonite suitcases filled with all the gifts and clothes we would need for the trip, I thought back to the toilet girl.

I could have easily grown up in India, never even knowing what else was out there.

If my dad never left, if my parents never married, and if they never settled in the US...

I have my struggles, sure, but I every time I step back into India, I step back into a time where my life could have been different.

It always makes me wonder...

How was I chosen for my life?

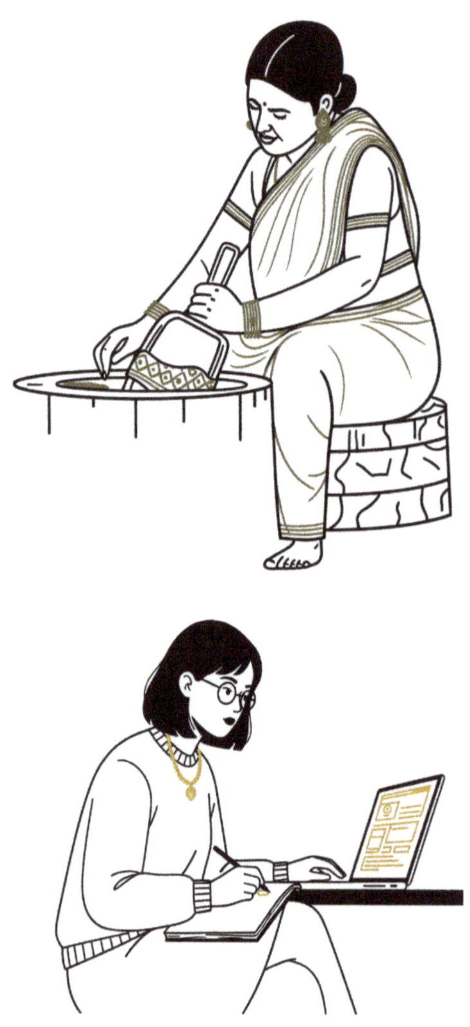

Desi Woman

Who is she?
The woman in the Delhi airport. Sweeping bathroom stalls.

Who is she?
The woman on the Colombo street. Selling sweet treats.

Who is she?
The woman at the Kolkata shop. Helping shoppers buy.

Who is she?
The women in the Karachi kitchen. Cooking in another's home.

Who is she?
The woman police officer. Solving New York City crimes.

Who is she?
The scholar. Grabbing accolades from the Boston boys.

Who is she?
The tech executive. Creating solutions in Silicon Valley.

Who is she?
The doctor. Saving lives in Chicago and ridding pain.

Who is she?
The athelete. Striving for a different type of gold for the USA.

Who is she?

The working *Desi* woman.
She does different jobs,
She lives different lives,
And yet she marks her future just the same.

The Dancer

She dances with *ghungru* on her feet.
Bells chime with every step.

She dances with her heart open.
Chest shining proud and strong.

She dances with expression.
Eyes lined with *kohl,* dance side to side.

She dances with her arms.
Outstretched and embracing.

She dances with her mind.
Thoughtful and practiced.

She dances telling tales of old,
Of gods, kings, flowers, and snakes.

Sometimes she dances for the crowds.
Smiling wide and strong.
Mostly she dances for herself.
Relishing every song.

She reaches out, hands steady and eyes calm.
She looks up, "sit down."
Gently examining soft fingers.
Her own fingers stained and brown.

She starts designing, hands working swiftly.
She looks down, as her fingers dance.
Listening to the world around her.
Her own words held inside.

She sits straight, neck aching.
She pauses for a sip, and a neck roll.
Counting designs per hand.
Her mind racing through sums.

The Henna
Artist

She continues working, fingers throbbing.
She is used to the pressure.
Designing hands covered in gold.
While her hands bear only stains.

She sits still,
while the others dance and eat,
She sits still,
while others talk and sing,
She sits still,
and listens to young and old.

Despite the changing time or place.
Her eyes stay kind and calm.
Despite the work she has to do.
Her hands stay steady and true.

Heroine

She's never sorry for who she is,
She rises to the occasion.

She's never sad about her status,
She stands tall everywhere.

She's not hurting over inequity,
She continues to march on.

She's not closed to the world,
She keeps her heart open.

She is not afraid of what may be,
She lives in today.

She is not quiet in the storm,
She speaks her mind freely.

As she creates her worth,
she raises yours.

She is my hero.

*(Go ahead, screenshot this and
send it to your heroine!)*

Farewell

I will never sleep the same.

Sleepless from their cries and movements.
Their need is real.
"Feed them every 3 hours."
Sealing them and me.

Sleepless from their protests,
Sleep regressions are no joke.
"Let them cry for at least 5 minutes."
5 excruciating minutes.

Sleepless from their midnight wakes,
And cuddles.
"Let them sleep. Let me sleep."
Just 10 more minuties.

Sleepless from thier absence,
As they grow and mature.
"They grow up so fast."
Stay young a bit longer.

Sleepless when they are out,
Worries and stress.
"They are grown up."
Don't grow up too fast.

I bid farewell to my dear sleep.
Lost years ago with new birth.
Replaced with an unending yawn,
Mixed with a dash of devotion.

four:
jaan
(heart)

Commentary to reflect on and renew oneself. Use of the word *jaan* is usually retained for those closest to you, who hold space in your heart.

Subah
(morning)

It shines
   upon you,
Asking you to
   shine too.

And it asks you to wash away...

Your night,
Your week.
Your darkness...
   and refresh your view.

As you arise,
   and stretch out,
Your whole self
   to begin anew.

Our Mothers

Some mothers are born.
Through birth and carriage.

Others are inherited.
Through contract and marriage.

Some mothers are bread.
Through time and earth.

Others are adopted.
Through support and dearth.

Some mothers tried to be.
Through trials and grief.

Others had only a moment.
No matter how brief.

Despite the ways our mothers came to be.
Their role is tried and true.
They build us up with space to thrive,
Like no others do.

Golden Girl

You know the type.

Jet black hair.
Brown chai skin.
Kohl-lined eyes.
Ears pierced with dangles.

Dangles of gold.
The goldest gold.

Not American gold.

You know the type.

Rose water scent.
Bright *bandhani* clothes.
Sparkly sandals.
Bracelets that jingle.

Jingles of gold.
The goldest gold.

You know the type.

Women forged by spice and fire.
Molded by culture and time.
Women built strong and proud to be.
Women who sparkle and shine.

What I am

I am my mother's daughter.
I cook before I think.
I crave ideation and creation.
I show care through my acts.

I am my fathers daughter.
I debate and discuss.
I relish science and literature.
I rule with a soft fist.

I am my parents daughter.
I hold their culture and tradition.
I pave my own path.
I strive to build better.

I am not sure who I thought I would be.
I never imagined my type.
I reacted and rebelled.
I retained and I restoried.

I am their best version of me.

Imperfect

Half the time
  Things seem funny.
Laughter is resounding.
The walls fill
  Up and into it.

Life seems so sweet.

Half the time
  Life envelopes us.
Bitterness and tears.
As those walls
  Close in.

The outside world turns dark.

No longer bright souls,
Void with laughter lost.

Evolution

Fitness was not a common thing.
So exercise did not come easy.

Running was only for gym class.
So walking was her pace.

Strength was for the boys.
So weights were never lifted.

Until she changed.

She picked up a dumbell.
And felt stronger than ever.

She ran on the treadmill.
And let her lungs fill in.

She found a love for movement.
And craved that endorphin high.

Fitness was not a common thing,
And she never knew the why.

Eventually, though she found it her way,
And it changed her day by day.

Looking Glass

I live to observe.
Always have, always will.
Some observations stay,
Seered in.

From staring out car windows.
Or through traincar bars.
Imagining their lives.
And who they wish to be.

The woman walking on a dirt road,
carrying wood on her head.
Where is she going?
Who taught her to carry?
So straight, no tettering.

What does she dream of?

The man guiding the buffalo cart through my
grandmother's town.
What is his work?
Are they his?

What does he seek to achieve?

The child begging on the roadside.
One leg full, one a stump.
What does his future hold?
Who holds him?

What hope does he carry?

I live to observe.
Always have, always will.
Some observations stay,
Forever seered in.

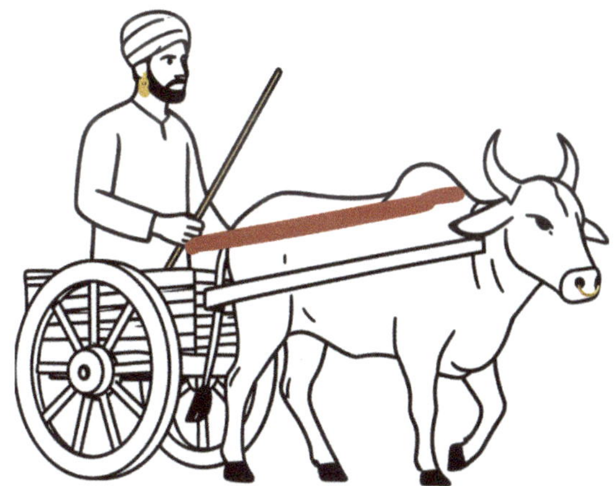

Pranayama

At times...

Breathing can feel hard...
In the dark spaces of your mind.
You breathe in sorrow, grief, and sadness.
One breath in, for one breath out.

Breathing can be healing...
In the grey shadows of your heart.
You breathe in calm, rest, and reset.
Two breaths in, for one breath out.

Breathing can be joyful,
In the bright corners of your eyes.
You breathe in energy, awareness, and light.
Three breaths in, for one breath out.

Breathing can bring change...
Pain and healing, turn to light.
Breathing towards better.
Refilling with resolve.

"Om"

The sights
   And stories...
Coming to life.

Moments of peace.
   A breath.
   A sound.
   A feeling.

One big bang.

Never heard, but often recited.
Never said, but often spoken.
Never felt, but often experienced.
Never seen, but giving life every day.

Duality

Worlds intersect...
Work and Play.
Culture and Heritage.
Money and Passion.
Immigrant and American.

Melding patterns.

Patterns of hope.
Patterns of confusion.
Patterns of reflection.
Patterns of privilege.

Combining and contradicting.

Contradicting life.
Contradicting purpose.
Contradicting goals.
Contradicting passion.

Causing chaos.
Raising calm.

Calm to do both.
Calm to be both.
Calm to accept both.
Calm to be.

The (new) Good Brown Girls

You have heard of the girls with their heads held high.
Shrouded by choice.
Covered by no one.

You have heard of the girls who truly love chai.
Serving by choice.
Pressured by no one.

You have heard of the girls who carry their culture.
Wearing with pride.
Picking their looks.

You have heard of the girls who shatter ceilings.
Rising their own way.
Lifting others around them.

You have heard of the girls who know their worth.
Choosing their path.
Not letting others define them.

You have heard of these girls.
They are deep in you.
They are the girls who drive change.
And help to retain.
They are the girls who bring light.
By lettings others shine.

They are **Good Brown Girls**.

five:
katham
(the end)

In the end, the circle
of life starts again.

Katham means finished, done, or
complete. And though we may
not be done, we are for now.

About this
Collection

It began again one day, after a wedding, when I was peeling off my prickly blouse and pulling out my heavy *jhumkas*. I had to write the feelings (physical and emotional) down, and I knew who could relate.

I was the girl at the wedding.
I am the girl at the wedding.
Or she was a version of me.

This is a collection of stories of other women as well. The women may or may not be known to me, but are known somewhere.

And, there is a common thread.
The stories we tell, or don't tell, matter.
The things we feel matter.
The things we never say out loud matter.

I hope this book can be something to help us all grow stronger in ourselves. To speak the unspeakable. To do the unthinkable. To charter the course many of our mothers did, in our own way.

For those not identifying as brown women, there is space for your own story within these pages as well.

If you seek to find it.

About Parul

Parul Bhandari is an author, speaker, and experience consultant. She became an author with the launch of her children's book, **Shine a Light on Diwali,** which showcases her experience celebrating Diwali as a first generation Indian born in America with her family.

Since then, Parul has continued to publish books which preserve, retell, and renew multi-cultural stories, for a modern audience.

She focuses heavily on American-born Indian stories due to her heritage, but has extended to some fictional depth as well.

In addition to her writing, Parul coaches other writers and creatives (like her 7-year old son who became a two-time author), through workshops and other activities.

Parul lives In Chicago with her husband and two sons.

Learn more at: www.parullbhandari.com

Keep up with Parul through her culture, heritage, and literature-focused work by subscribing to her newsletter.

Follow our family of work at
www.bhandaribooks.com

2024

2025

2025

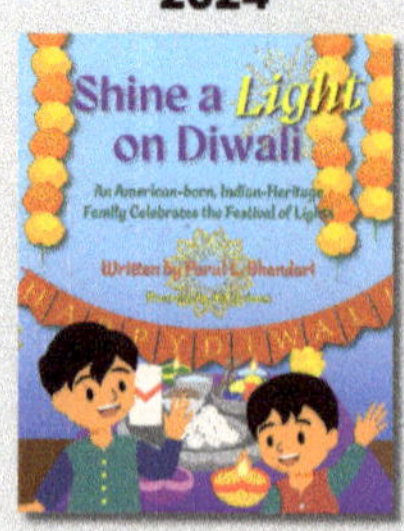

2025

2026

2026

2026/2027

Middle Grade Graphic Novel - planned for 2026

Travel Book - India planned 2026/2027

2025

2026

books written by 7-year old Jaiyen

www.ingramcontent.com/pod-product-compliance
Lightning Source LLC
Chambersburg PA
CBHW041645150726
48005CB00015BA/2401